JOE'S ELECTRONIC HANDBOOK

Joes Car

Capacitors trap DC current and let AC pass

Alternating current is usually produced by rotating a coil in a magnetic field
- AC voltage is usually specified at a value equal to the DC voltage capable of doing the same work
- This value is .707 times the peak voltage called the root mean square voltage
- The peak voltage (or current) is 1.41 times the RMS value

Electrical "Ground"
- One of the wires is connected by the earth by a metal rod. Metal enclosures of electricity power devices are connected to this <u>Ground</u> wire.This prevents a shock hazard should a non-grounded wire make contact with the metal enclosure.

Relays
- A relay is an electromagnetic switch. A small current flowing through a coil in the relay creates a magnetic field that pulls one switch contact against or away from another

<u>Diagram: Symbol of Relay (point contact)</u>

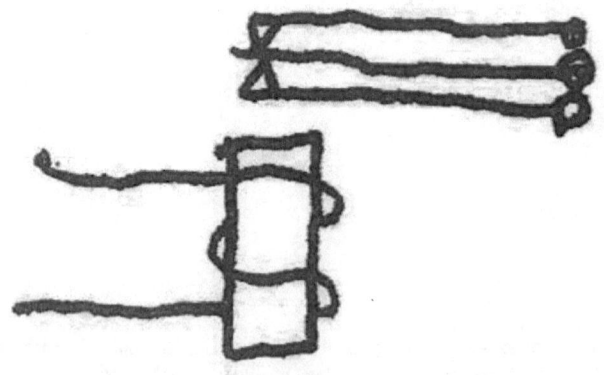

Choke

- o Used in many circuits to limit or suppress fluctuating
  signals while passing a steady current.

Transformers

- ○ Isolation transformer has 1:1 ratio
- ○ Step up transformer has 1:5 ratio
- ○ Step down transformer has 5:1 ratio

Diagram of waves

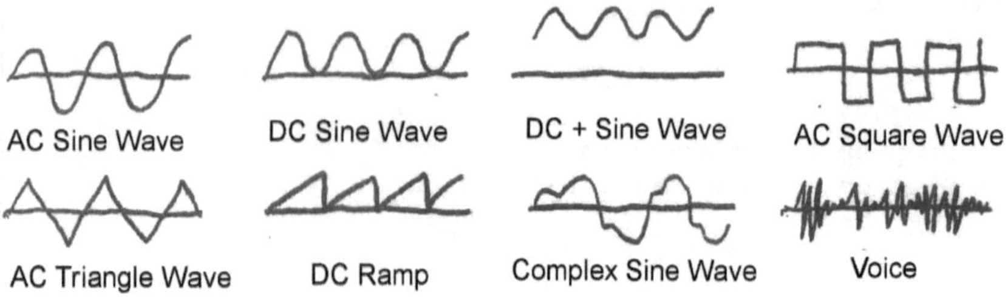

AC Sine Wave

DC Sine Wave

DC + Sine Wave

AC Square Wave

AC Triangle Wave

DC Ramp

Complex Sine Wave

Voice

Diagram: Coil Current Flow Waves

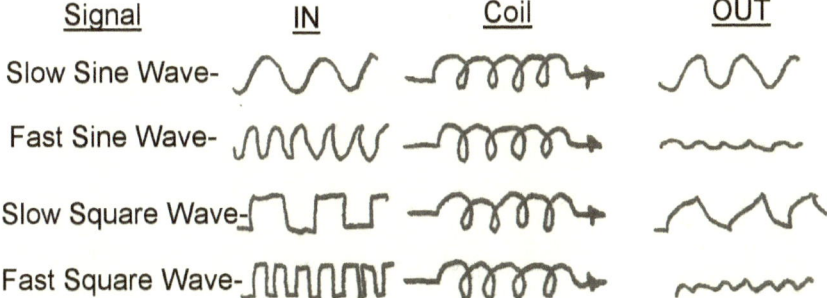

Signal	IN	Coil	OUT

Slow Sine Wave-

Fast Sine Wave-

Slow Square Wave-

Fast Square Wave-

Diodes

Small signal
- o Small signal diodes are used to transform low current AC to DC, Detect (demodulate) radio signals, multiply voltage, perform logic, absorb voltage spikes, etc.

Power rectifiers
- o Functionally identical to small signal diodes, power rectifiers can handle <u>much</u> more current.

Zener
- o The zener diode is designed to have a specific reverse breakdown (conduction) voltage. This means zener diodes can function like a voltage sensitive switch.

Light emitting
- o All diodes emit some electromagnetic radiation when forward based. Diodes made from certain semiconductors (like gallium arsenide phosphide) emit considerably more radiation than silicon diodes. These are called light emitting diodes or LED

Photodiode
- o All diodes respond to some degree when illuminated. Diodes designed specifically to detect light are called photodiodes.

Transistors (bipolar)

Small signal
o Small signal transistors are used to amplify low level signals

Power
o Power transistors are used in high power amplifiers and power supplies

High-frequency-
o High-frequency transistors operated at radio, television, and microwave frequencies

<u>Diagram: Bipolar Transistors</u>

 - small signal and switching

   - power

  - high frequency

How bipolar transistors work

Switch

- When the base of a NPN transistor is grounded (0 volts), no current flows from the emitter to the collector
  - Transistor is "off"

- If the base is forward-biased by at least 0.6 volts, a current will flow from the emitter to the collector
  - Transistor is "on"

Amplifier

- If the base is forward-biased, the emitter-collector current will flow variations in a much smaller base current.

JFETS (Junction Field - Effect Transistors)

- Two kinds of Jfets
  - N-Channel

o P-Channel

The channel is like a silicon resistor that conducts current moving from the source to the drain.

A voltage at the gate increases the channel resistence and reduces drain source current.

An Jfet can be considered an amplifier and switch

Transistors (JFET)

Small signal and switching

o Small signal JFETs are used at the input stage of amplifiers to provide a high resistance input. They are also used a switches.

High frequency

o High frequency JFETs are used to amplify or produce
   high frequency signals

Transistors (MOSFET)

Mosfet operation

o All mosfet are N-type or P-type. Unline the junction,
   Fet, the gate of a mostfet has <u>no</u> electrical contact
   with source and drain.

o A positive gate voltage attracts electrons to the
   region below the gate

o The gate voltage determines the resistance of the
   channel

Transistors (Unijunction)

o The unijunction transistor (ujt) is not a true
   transistor. It's more like a adiode with two cathode
   connections. It works like a voltage-controlled switch
   and does amp.

o UJT operation

   o Usually a small current will flow from base 1 to
      base 2. When the voltage applied to the emitter
      reaches a certain threshold (several volts), the
      UJT switches on and a high current flows from
      base 1 to the emitter below the threshold
      voltage, no current flows from base 1 to the
      emitter.

Silicon-controlled rectifiers (scrs)

o The scr is similar to a bipolar transistor with a
   fourth layer sometimes called a 4-layer PNPN diode
   since it passes current in only on direction

SCR operation

- o If the anode of an scr is made more positive than the earthode the two outermost PN junctions are forward biased. The middle junction is reversed biased which allows a much larger current to flow through the device.

Triacs

- o The triac is equivalent to two SCRs connected in parallel. This means triacs can switch both direct and alternating current. The triac has 5 layers

Triac operation

- o When used to switch alternating current, the triac stays on when the gate pecreves current

- o Triacs, like scrs, are categorized according to the current they can switch. Triacs don't have very high power capabilities.

LEDs

o The light emmited by an incandescent lamp contains many wavelengths. The light emitted by an LED has a narrow wavelength range.

o Too much current will overheat the led and possibly separate the leads or melt the semiconductor chip

o The light emmited by an LED is directly proportioned to current through the LED. This means LEDs are ideal for transmitting information.

Diagram: Electromagnetic spectrum

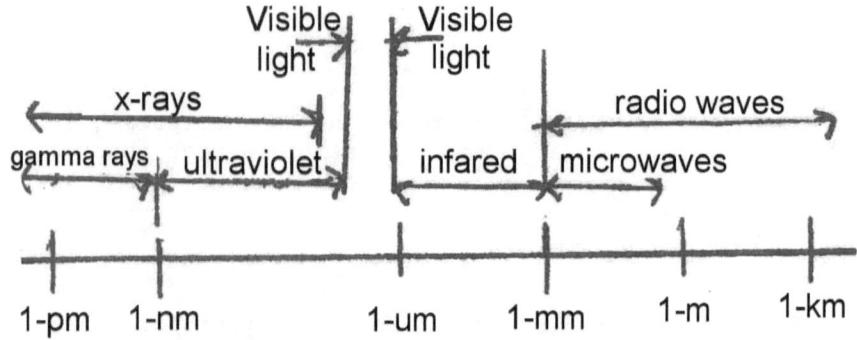

1pm = 1 picometer
1nm = 1 nanometer
1um = 1 micrometer
1mm = 1 millimeter
1m = 1 meter
1km = 1 kilometer

Diagram: Forward voltage and wavelength of an LED

Wavelenth (mm)	Voltage
565 (green)	2.2-3.0
590 (yellow)	2.2-3.0
615 (orange)	1.8-2.7
640 (red)	1.6-2.0
690 (red)	2.2-3.0
880 (infared)	2.0-2.5
900 (infared)	1.2-1.6
940 (infared)	1.3-1.7

Visibile light leds
   o These inexpensive leds are used as indicator light

Led displays
   o Many kinds of led read outs capable of displaying
     digits and characters are available. They are more
     rugged than liquid crystal displays, but they use more
     current.

Infared Leds
  o They are used to transmit information

Required series resistance formula
  o Protect from excessive current
  o Rs= (Supply voltage-LED Voltage)/LED Current

IC's

  o Analog (or linear) IC's produce, amplify or respond to variable voltages. Analog IC's include many kinds of amplifiers, timers, oscillators and voltage regulators

  o Digital (or logic) IC's respond to or produce signals having only two voltage levels. Digital IC's include microprocessors, memories, microcomputers and many kinds of smaller chips.

Diagram: IC's specifications

Voltage

Time

Analog IC's

Digital IC's

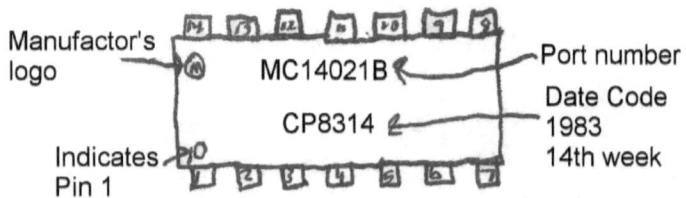

Manufactor's logo

Indicates Pin 1

MC14021B

CP8314

Port number

Date Code
1983
14th week

Diagram Gates

"AND" gate

A B	Out
L L	L
L H	L
H L	L
H H	H

"Or" gate

A B	Out
L L	L
L H	H
H L	H
H H	H

"Not" gate

In	Out
L	H
H	L

"Nand" gate

A B	Out
L L	H
L H	H
H L	H
H H	L

"Nor" gate

A B	Out
L L	H
L H	L
H L	L
H H	L

Exclusive "or" gate

A B	Out
L L	L
L H	H
H L	H
H H	L

Exclusive "nor" gate

A B	Out
L L	H
L H	L
H L	L
H H	L

3 input "out" gate

A B C	Out
L L L	L
L L H	L
L H L	L
L H H	L
H L L	L
H L H	L
H H L	L
H H H	H

3 input "nand" gate

A B C	Out
L L L	H
L L H	H
L H L	H
L H H	H
H L L	H
H L H	H
H H L	H
H H H	L

* 9 7 8 1 5 1 1 7 8 1 8 7 9 *